·THE·
·BABY'S·OPERA·

·KING·COLE·

THE
BABY'S·OPERA·

A
BOOK·OF·OLD
RHYMES·WITH
NEW·DRESSES
BY

THE·MUSIC·BY
THE·EARLIEST
MASTERS

WALTER·CRANE;

Windmill Books/Simon & Schuster
New York

Published 1981 by Windmill Books, Inc. and
Simon & Schuster, a Division of Gulf & Western Corporation
Simon & Schuster Building
1230 Avenue of the Americas
New York, New York 10020
Published by arrangement with Pan Books, London
WINDMILL BOOKS and colophon are trademarks of Windmill Books, Inc.,
registered in the United States Patent and Trademark Office.
Manufactured in the United States of America
10 9 8 7 6 5 4 3 2 1

Library of Congress Cataloging in Publication Data

Crane, Walter, 1845–1915.
The baby's opera.

Reprint of the 190-? ed. published by F. Warne,
London and New York.
For piano, with interlinear words.
SUMMARY: An illustrated collection of nursery
rhymes set to music.
1. Children's songs.   2. Nursery rhymes—Musical
settings. [1. Songs.   2. Nursery rhymes]   I. Title.
M1997.C89B3 1981   784.6′2406   80-28586
ISBN 0-671-42551-X

CONTENTS

1 { Girls and boys come out to play, The
  { Leave your sup - per, and leave your sleep;

moon doth shine as bright as day; {
Come to your playfellows in the street; { 2. { Come with a whoop, and
                                              { Up the lad-der and

come with a call, Come with a good will or not at all. }
down the wall, A pen - ny loaf will serve you all. }

9

THE MVL-BERRY BVSH

Here we go round the mul-berry bush, the mul-berry bush, the mulberry bush;

Here we go round the mulberry bush, All on a fros-ty morn - ing.

This is the way we clap our hands, This is the way we clap our hands,

This is the way we clap our hands, All on a fros-ty morn - ing.

II

ORANGES & LEMONS

Oran-ges and le mons, says the bells of St. Clemen's; You owe me five farthings, says the

D.C. When will that be? says the bells of Step - ney; I do not know, says the

bells of St. Mar -tin's; When will you pay me, says the bells of Old Bai - ley;

great bell of Bow.

When I grow rich, says the bells of Shore - ditch; Here comes a can-dle to

light you to bed, And here comes a chop -per to chop off your head.

St. PAUL'S STEEPLE

Up - on Paul's stee - ple stands a tree As full of ap - ples as may be, The

lit - tle boys of Lon - don town They run with hooks to pull them down; And

then they run from hedge to hedge Un - til they come to Lon - don Bridge.

·NATURAL·HISTORY·

1. What are lit - tle boys made of?
2. What are lit - tle girls made of?

What are lit - tle boys made of? Frogs and snails and
What are lit - tle girls made of? Su - gar and spice and

pup - py-dog's tails, And that are lit - tle boys made of.
all that's nice, And that are lit - tle girls made of.

3. What are young men made of?
What are young men made of?
Sighs and leers, and crocodile tears,
And that are young men made of.

4. What are young women made of?
What are young women made of?
Ribbons and laces, and sweet pretty faces,
And that are young women made of.

16

·LAVENDER'S·BLVE·

La - ven - der's blue, did-dle, did-dle! La - ven - der's green;

When I am king, did-dle. diddle! You shall be queen.

2. Call up your men, diddle, diddle!
   Set them to work;
   Some to the plough, diddle, diddle!
   Some to the cart.

3. Some to make hay, diddle, diddle!
   Some to cut corn;
   While you and I, diddle, diddle!
   Keep ourselves warm.

I SAW THREE SHIPS

1. I saw three ships come sail - ing by,
2. And what do you think was in them then,

Sail - ing by, sail - ing by, I saw three ships come
In them then, in them then, And what do you think was

sail - ing by, On New-year's Day in the morn - - ing.
in them then, On New-year's Day in the morn - - ing?

3. Three pretty girls were in them then,
   In them then, in them then,
   Three pretty girls were in them then,
   On New-year's Day in the morning.

4. And one could whistle, and one could sing,
   The other play on the violin;
   Such joy there was at my wedding,
   On New-year's Day in the morning.

I·SAW· ·THREE·SHIPS·

DING·DONG·BELL

Ding dong bell! Pus-sy's in the well! Who put her in? Lit-tle Tommy Lin.

Who pulled her out? Lit-tle Tommy Stout. What a naughty boy was that To

drown poor pussy-cat, Who ne'er did any harm, But killed all the mice in fa-ther's barn.

·PUSS · AT · COURT·

"Pus - sy - cat, pus - sy - cat, where have you been?"   "I've been to Lon - don to look at the Queen."   "Pus - sy - cat, pus - sy - cat, what did you there?"   "I caught a lit - tle mouse un - der the chair."

Three blind mice,... See how they run! They all ran af-ter the farmer's wife, Who cut off their tails with a car-ving knife; Did e-ver you hear such a thing in your life?.... Three blind mice...

• DICKORY • DOCK •

Hick - o - ry, dick - o - ry dock! . . . . The mouse ran

up the clock; . . . . The clock struck one, The

mouse ran down, Hick - o - ry, dick - o - ry dock! . . . .

2.

The frog he would a-wooing ride, Heigh-ho, &c.
Sword and buckler at his side, With a, &c.

3.

When upon his high horse set, Heigh-ho, &c.
His boots they shone as black as jet, With a, &c.

4.

When he came to the merry mill-pin, Heigh-ho, &c.
"Lady Mouse, are you within?" With a, &c.

5.

Then came out the dusty mouse, Heigh-ho, &c
"I am the lady of this house," With a, &c.

6.

"Hast thou any mind of me?" Heigh-ho, &c.
"I have e'en great mind of thee," With a, &c.

7.

"Who shall this marriage make?" Heigh-ho, &c.
"Our lord, which is the rat," With a, &c.

8.

"What shall we have to our supper?" Heigh-ho, &c.
"Three beans in a pound of butter," With a, &c.

9.

But when the supper they were at, Heigh-ho, &c.
The frog, the mouse, and e'en the rat, With a, &c.

10

Then came in Tib, our cat, Heigh-ho, &c.
And caught the mouse e'en by the back, With a, &c

11.

Then did they separate, Heigh-ho, &c.
The frog leaped on the floor so flat, With a, &c.

12.

Then came in Dick, our drake, Heigh-ho, &c.
And drew the frog e'en to the lake, With a, &c.

13.

The rat he ran up the wall, Heigh-ho, &c.
And so the company parted all, With a, &c

2. " O ! there is sweet music on yonder green
    hill, O !
    And you shall be a dancer, **a dancer in**
    yellow,
    All in yellow, all in yellow."
    Said the crow to the frog, and then, O !
    " All in yellow, all in yellow,"
    Said the frog to the crow again, O !

3. " Farewell, ye little fishes, that in the river
    swim, O !
    I'm going to be a dancer, a dancer in yel-
    low."
    " O beware ! O beware !"
    Said the fish to the frog, and then, O !
    " I'll take care, I'll take care,"
    Said the frog to the fish again, O !

4. The frog began a swimming, a swimming
    to land, O !
    And the crow began jumping to give him
    his hand, O !
    " Sir, you're welcome, Sir, you're welcome,"
    Said the crow to the frog, and then, O !
    " Sir, I thank you, Sir, I thank you,"
    Said the frog to the crow, again, O !

5. " But where is the sweet music on yonder
    green hill, O ?
    And where are all the dancers, the dancers
    in yellow ?
    All in yellow, all in yellow ?"
    Said the frog to the crow, and then, O !
    " Sir, they're here, Sir, they're here,"
    Said the crow to the frog—*

* Here the crow swallows the frog.

MRS BOND

1. "Oh, what have you got for din-ner, Mrs. Bond?" "There's beef in the lar-der, and ducks in the pond;" "Dil-ly, dil-ly, dil-ly, dil-ly, come to be killed, For you must be stuffed, and my cus-to-mers filled!"

2. "John Ostler, go fetch me a duckling or two,
   John Ostler go fetch me a duckling or two;
   Cry dilly, dilly, dilly, dilly, come and be killed,
   For you must be stuffed, and my customers filled!"

3. "I have been to the ducks that are swimming in the pond,
   And they won't come to be killed, Mrs. Bond;
   I cried dilly, dilly, dilly, dilly, come and be killed,
   For you must be stuffed, and the customers filled!"

4. Mrs. Bond she went down to the pond in a rage,
   With plenty of onions, and plenty of sage;
   She cried, "Come, little wag-tails, come, and be killed,
   For you shall be stuffed, and my customers filled!"

MRS BOND

THE TAKE INN

XMAS DAY IN Yᵉ MORNING

1. Dame, get up and bake your pies, Bake your
2. Dame, what makes your maid - ens lie, Maid - ens

pies, bake your pies; Dame, get up and
lie, maid - ens lie? Dame, what makes your

bake your pies, On Christ - mas - day in the morn - - ing.
maid - ens lie, On Christ - mas - day in the morn - - ing?

3. Dame, what makes your ducks to die,
Ducks to die, ducks to die?
Dame, what makes your ducks to die,
On Christmas-day in the morning?

4. Their wings are cut, they cannot fly,
Cannot fly, cannot fly;
Their wings are cut, they cannot fly,
On Christmas-day in the morning.

30

KING ARTHUR

1. When good King Ar-thur ruled this land, He was a good-ly king— He stole three pecks of bar-ley-meal, To make a bag pud-ding.

2. A bag pudding the Queen did make,
   And stuffed it well with plums,
   And in it put great lumps of fat
   As big as my two thumbs.

3. The King and Queen did eat thereof,
   And noblemen beside,
   And what they could not eat that night
   The Queen next morning fried.

Y^e · GOOD · KING · ARTHVR ·

33

Ye JOLLY MiLLER

There was a jol-ly mil-ler once Lived on the ri-ver Dee;.... He
worked and sang from morn till night, No lark more blithe than he...... And
this the bur-den of his song For e-ver used to be,........ "I
care for no-bo-dy, no, not I, And no-bo-dy cares for me."....

34

Yᵉ SONG oF SIXPENCE

1. Sing a song of six - pence, a pocket full of rye ; Four and twenty black - birds baked in a pie ; When the pie was o - pen the birds be-gan to sing, Was-n't that a dain-ty dish to set be-fore the king?

2. The king was in his counting-house counting out his money ;
The queen was in the parlour eating bread and honey ;
The maid was in the garden hanging out her clothes,
When up came a blackbird and pecked off her nose.

1. Lit-tle Bo-Peep, she lost her sheep, And did-n't know
where to find them; Let them a-lone, they'll
all come home And bring their tails be-hind them.

2. Little Bo-Peep fell fast asleep,
   And dreamt she heard them bleating;
   But when she awoke, she found it a joke,
   For they were still a-fleeting.

3. Then up she took her little crook,
   Determined for to find them,
   She found them indeed, but it made her
        heart bleed
   For they'd left their tails behind them.

4. It happened one day as Bo-Peep did stray
   Into a meadow hard by,
   There she espied their tails side by side,
   All hung on a tree to dry.

5. She heaved a sigh and wiped her eye,
   Then went o'er hill and dale,
   And tried what she could, as a shep-
        herdess should,
   To tack to each sheep its tail.

36

‧BAA!‧ ‧BAA! BLACK‧SHEEP‧

"Baa! Baa! Black sheep, have you a-ny wool?" "Yes, mar-ry,

have I, three bags full; One for my mas-ter, and

one for my dame, But none for the lit-tle boy that lives down the lane!"

TOM, THE PIPER'S SON

Tom, Tom, the pi-per's son, Stole a pig and a - way did run; The
pig was eat, and Tom was beat, And Tom went roar-ing down the street.

1. There was a la-dy loved a swine, "Ho - ney!" said she;
2. "I'll build thee a sil - ver sty, Ho - ney!" said she;

"Pig - hog, wilt thou be mine?" "Hunc!" said he.
"And in it thou shalt lie!" "Hunc!" said he.

3. " Pinned with a silver pin,
    Honey!" said she ;
    " That thou mayest go out and in,"
    " Hunc!ᴬ said he.

4. " Will thou have me now,
    Honey?" said she ;
    " Speak, or my heart will break,"
    " Hunc!" said he.

THERE WAS A LADY LOVED A SWINE

41

OVER·THE·HILLS·&·FAR·AWAY·

1. Tom he was a piper's son, He learnt to play when he was young; But all the tunes that he could play Was "O-ver the hills and far a-way."

O-ver the hills and a great way off, The wind shall blow my top-knot off.

2. Tom with his pipe made such a noise
That he pleased both the girls and boys,
And they stopped to hear him play,
"Over the hills and far away."
Over the hills, &c.

COCK ROBIN AND JENNY WREN

1. 'Twas on a mer-ry time, When Jenny Wren was young. So neat-ly as she danced, And so sweet-ly as she sung, Rob-in Redbreast lost his heart, He was a gallant bird, He doffed his cap to Jenny Wren, Requesting to be heard.

2. "My dearest Jen-ny Wren, If you will but be mine, You shall dine on cher-ry pie, And drink nice currant wine; I'll dress you like a gold-finch, Or like a peacock gay, So if you'll have me. Jenny, dear, Let us appoint the day."

3. Jenny blushed behind her fan
And thus declared her mind —
"So let it be to-morrow, Rob,
"I'll take your offer kind;
"Cherry pie is very good,
"And so is currant wine;
"But I will wear my plain brown gown,
"And never dress too fine."

4. Robin Redbreast got up early,
All at the break of day,
He flew to Jenny Wren's house,
And sang a roundelay;
He sang of Robin Redbreast,
And pretty Jenny Wren,
And when he came unto the end,
He then began again.

I HAD·A·LITTLE· NVT·TREE

I had a lit-tle nut-tree, no-thing would it bear But a sil-ver nut-meg and a gold-en pear; The King of Spain's daughter came to vi-sit me, And all for the sake of my lit-tle nut-tree.

I HAD A LITTLE   NVT TREE

DR. FAVSTVS

Doc-tor Faus-tus was a good man, He whipt his scho-lars now and then;

When he whipt he made them dance Out of Eng-land in-to France;

Out of France in-to Spain, And then he whipt them back a-gain.

THREE CHILDREN

1. Three chil - dren sli - - ding on the ice, All on a sum - mer's day,........ As it fell out, they all fell in, The rest they ran a - way........

2. Now, had these children been at home,
    Or sliding on dry ground,
Ten thousand pounds to one penny,
    They had not all been drowned.

3. You parents all that children have,
    And you that have got none,
If you would have them safe abroad,
    Pray keep them safe at home.

MY·PRETTY·MAID·

1. "Where are you going to, my pret-ty maid? Where are you going to,

my pretty maid?" "I'm go-ing a-milk-ing, Sir," she said,

"Sir," she said, "Sir," she said, "I'm go-ing a-milk-ing, Sir," she said.

2. "Shall I go with you, my pretty maid?"
   "Yes, if you please, kind Sir," she said,
   "Sir," she said, "Sir," she said,
   "Yes, if you please, kind Sir," she said.

3. "What is your fortune, my pretty maid?"
   "My face is my fortune, Sir," she said,
   "Sir," she said, "Sir," she said,
   "My face is my fortune, "Sir," she said.

4. "Then I can't marry you, my pretty maid."
   "Nobody asked you, Sir," she said,
   "Sir," she said, "Sir," she said,
   "Nobody asked you, Sir," she said.

49

·THE·PLOVGH·BOY·IN·LVCK·

1. My dad-dy is dead, but I can't tell you how; He left me six hor-ses to fol-low the plough: With my whim wham wad-dle ho! Strim stram strad-dle ho! Bub-ble ho! pret-ty boy, o-ver the brow.

2. I sold my six horses to buy me a cow;
   And wasn't that a pretty thing to follow
   the plough?   With my, &c.

3. I sold my cow to buy me a calf,
   For I never made a bargain but I lost the
   best half.   With my, &c.

4. I sold my calf to buy me a cat,
   To sit down before the fire to warm her
   little back.   With my, &c.

5. I sold my cat to buy me a mouse,
   But she took fire in her tail and so burnt
   up my house.   With my, &c.

·WARM·HANDS·

Warm hands, warm, the men are gone to plough;

If you want to warm your hands, warm your hands now.

Jack and Jill went up the hill To fetch a pail of wa - ter; Jack fell down and broke his crown, And Jill came tum - bling af - ter.

JACK & JILL.

Dance a ba - by did - dy!..... What can
mam - my do wid - 'e?...... Sit in her lap,
Give it some pap, And dance a ba - by did - dy!....

Grandmothers
Are
Special People

Edited by Jill Wolf

Photographs by Terry Donnelly

ISBN 0-89954-445-2

Photographs © Terry Donnelly
Text copyright © 1993 Antioch Publishing Company

Yellow Springs, Ohio 45387
Printed in the U.S.A.

CONTENTS

It is as grandmothers that our mothers
come into the fullness of their grace.

— Christopher Morley

The grandchildren were always
delighted to see her . . .

— Peregrine Churchill

Some of the world's best educators
are grandparents.

— *Charles W. Shedd*

 THE FULLNESS OF YOUR GRACE

Grandmothers Are Special People

Grandmothers are special people;
They're one of life's warmest joys,
Because their giving extends beyond
Cookies and childhood toys.
They're teachers, guides,
    and role models
For what we aspire to do;
They're friends who cross
    the gap of years,
They're second mothers, too.
Because they've lived so fully,
They have so much to share—
Stories, dreams, and memories,
The patience to listen and care,
A hug for all the good things we do,
A handkerchief for the tears,
Laughter and smiles for silly things,
Prayers and advice for our fears.
Grandmothers are special people;
They have this wonderful way
Of letting us know we're special, too,
And loved each and every day.

—*Jill Wolf*

A grandam's name is little less in love
Than is the doting title of a mother.

—*William Shakespeare*

What is better than gold?
  Jasper.
What is better than jasper?
  Wisdom.
What is better than wisdom?
  Women.
And what is better than a good woman?
  Nothing.

— Geoffrey Chaucer

Honor women! They entwine and weave
heavenly roses in our earthly life.

—*Johann von Schiller*

A good woman is said to resemble a
Cremona violin—age but increases its
worth and sweetens its tone.

—*Oliver Wendell Holmes*

Beautiful young people are accidents of
nature. But beautiful old people are
works of art.

—*Marjorie Barstow Greenbie*

It is as grandmothers that our mothers come into the fullness of their grace. When a man's mother holds his child in her gladdened arms he is aware of the roundness of life's cycle; of the mystic harmony of life's ways.

— Christopher Morley

May the Lord bless you . . . and may you live to see your children's children.

Psalm 128:6 (NIV)

Children's children are a crown to the aged, and parents are the pride of their children.

Proverbs 17:6 (NIV)

The closest friends I have made all through life
have been people who also grew up close to a
loved and loving grandmother or grandfather.
— *Margaret Mead*

Call That Love

I have been taught
All homage is due
Those much older than I,
And so I respect you,
Grandmother dear.

Call that manners.

But I have not been taught
The heart must fill and feel
Such tenderness for you.
And yet it does.

Call that love.

—Lois Wyse

If nothing is going well, call your
grandfather or grandmother.

—Italian Proverb

The Importance of Grandparents

The importance of grandparents in the life of little children is immeasurable. A young child with the good fortune to have grandparents nearby benefits in countless ways. It has a place to share its joys, its sorrows, to find a sympathetic and patient listener, to be loved.

A child without grandparents can feel the lack of roots and a lack of connectedness. It misses a chance to link up with the past. Questions and answers about the "old days" locate a child historically in his own small world. It provides a sense of inner security and a feeling of belonging.

—*Edward Wakin*

No one . . . who has not known that inestimable
privilege can possibly realize what good fortune it is
to grow up in a home where there are grandparents.

—*Suzanne LaFollette*

So Many Things

So many things we love are you, I can't
seem to explain except by little things,
but flowers and beautiful handmade
things—small stitches. So much of our
reading and thinking—so many sweet
customs and so much of our . . . well, our
religion. It is all *you*. I hadn't realized it
before. This is so vague but do you see a
little, dear Grandma? I want to thank you.

—*Anne Morrow Lindbergh*

When I'm a Grandma, Too

I hope when I'm a grandma, too,
My hands will find small jobs to do,
Like knitting sweaters, making toys,
And gingerbread men for little boys,
A doll to dress for a small girl
And flaxen hair to softly curl.

I hope I have a doughnut crock
And red-striped peppermints in stock,
White aprons trimmed
    with homemade lace,
A kitten by the fireplace,
A hob to set a kettle on,
With rosy curtains snugly drawn.

I hope that I shall have a yard,
Where crimson hollyhocks stand guard
Near a small bed of mignonette,
That I shall have small meals to get,
Using my Sunday chinaware
With roses on the bill of fare.

That children, as they come along,
Will sense somehow that they belong
To all the beauty gathered here,
And feel themselves beloved and dear,
Beyond all language to convey,
Sheltered and guarded at their play.
I hope that I shall prove to be
All that they ever hoped of me.

—*Edna Jaques*

Grandma

My grandma likes to play with God,
They have a kind of game.
She plants the garden full of seeds,
He sends the sun and rain.

She likes to sit and talk with God
And knows He is right there.
She prays about the whole wide world,
Then leaves us in His care.

—Ann Johnson

MY HEART'S HOME

Grandma's House

Grandma's house is special,
And when we go to visit
We never have to phone ahead;
She doesn't ask, "Who is it?"

She somehow seems to know it's us,
And that we love to come,
For visiting at Grandma's house
Is lots more fun than home.

It isn't just the cookies,
Or the different toys we get—
It's not just fun with grandpa,
Or the dog and cat to pet.

It's not just snuggling quietly,
And rocking in her chair—
But Grandma's house is special
Because my grandma's there.

—Marian Benedict Manwell

Afternoon with Grandmother

I always shout when Grandma comes,
But Mother says, "Now please be still
And good and do what *Grandma* wants."
And I say, "Yes, I will."

So off we go in Grandma's car.
"There's a brand new movie
   quite near by,"
She says, "that I'd rather like to see."
And I say, "So would I."

The show has horses and chases
   and battles;
We gasp and hold hands the
   whole way through.
She smiles and says, "I liked that lots."
And I say, "I did, too."

"It's made me hungry, though," she says,
"I'd like a malt and tarts with jam.
By any chance are you hungry, too?"
And I say, "Yes, I am."

Later at home my mother says,
"I hope you were careful to do as bid.
Did you and grandma have a good time?"
And I say, "YES, WE DID!!!"

—*Barbara A. Huff*

Thanksgiving

"Home on Thanksgiving"
Is framed in my heart,
With turkeys and pumpkins
The happiest part.

Or perhaps my grandma
Was by far the best sight
With her flushed, happy face
When we ate with delight.

—*Helen Gingrich Knowlton*

Over the river and through the wood—
Now Grandmother's cap I spy!
Hurrah for the fun!
Is the pudding done?
Hurrah for the pumpkin-pie!

—*Lydia Maria Child*

The grandchildren were always delighted
to see her . . . They enjoyed her because
she obviously enjoyed them.

—*Peregrine Churchill*

The Road to Grandmother's

Ah, me, for the road that led away
Between the rows of the hedges tall,
With a stretch of haze low down
   in the west,
And a shimmer of clouds high over all.
And there were the fields
   of dreaming wheat
With a lark a-singing low in the grass,
With never a fear and never a care
For the passing by of a little lass.
And there was the breath of
   the clover blooms,
And the berry brambles a-reaching far,
But not so far as the heart of me
Reaching out where the
   dream worlds are.

And the road to Grandmother's led away
Straight on and on 'til it came to the sea,
With the white waves curling out
   in the bay,
And always a ship waiting there for me.
And I never knew to be tired then,
Nor weary at all when the day was done,
And I'd walk the road from
   Grandmother's home,
Blithe and gay at the set of sun.
Ah, the road in the morning was
   glad and fair,
But at night the light from the early star
Was a white ship bearing me
   home again
From the far countries where the
   dream worlds are.

— Grace Noll Crowell

Being grandparents sufficiently removes
us from the responsibilities so that we
can be friends—really good friends.
—*Allan Frome*

Grandparents are frequently more congenial with their grandchildren than with their children.

—*André Maurois*

Our grandchildren accept us for ourselves . . . as no one in our entire lives has ever done . . .

—*Ruth Goode*

Grandmother's Garden

In Grandma's special garden
There is always growing room,
Where wisdom, love, and patience
Bring everything to bloom.
Though she and Grandpa weed it
With faithfulness and care,
They like to leave wildflowers
Growing here and there.

There are columbines and roses,
Sweet lavender and thyme,
Purple morning glories
And pink sweet peas that climb.
There are clouds of baby's breath
And tiny coral bells,
Bright blue bachelor's buttons
And hollyhocks as well.

They call it Grandma's garden,
But it's Grandpa's garden, too,
And as they raised their flowers,
Their family also grew.
They tend their little garden
With a love that perseveres,
The kind of love they've given
To their family through the years.

—*Jill Wolf*

My Grandmother's Garden

My grandmother's garden,
  how well I remember!
The tall black-eyed susans
  that grew by the fence,
The ruby-red poppies that
  glowed like an ember,
And purple petunias with
  cinnamon scents.
I can still see the pond
  and the lilies around it;
I listen—and bird songs
  come calling to me.

And there was a pine tree—
  I know, for I found it—
Where summer winds whispered,
  unfettered and free.
The old stony pathways that ran
  through the arbor,
I traveled them all when I played
  as a child.
In sunshine and shadow I found
  a safe harbor—
A retreat for an hour,
  by cares undefiled.

At night, from my window,
  I'd throw back the shutter—
The moon washed with silver,
  my garden below,
The great summer moths from
  the shadows would flutter
And settle on rosebuds as white
  as the snow.
My grandmother's garden,
  once ringing with laughter,
Once filled with the voices
  of children at play—
I hope that my children, and all
  who come after
Will find such a garden—
  if just for a day!

—Hazel Werth

Great-Grandma's Flower Garden

The snowball bush in
　　Great-Grandma's yard
Drooping with heavy bloom,
Seemed to hold the winter's glory,
Leaving no trace of winter's gloom.

Peonies bloomed, pink, red and white,
Close to the picketed fence.
I liked the tulips and jonquils too,
And the blooming orchard scents.

A snowy shower of apple blossoms;
The porch banked with syringa's fluff;
Springtime in Great-Grandma's garden
Was a fairyland sure enough!

—Helen Gingrich Knowlton

If becoming a grandmother was only a matter of choice, I should advise every one of you straight way to become one. There is no fun . . . like it!

—*Hannah Whitall Smith*

The Spicebox

The many-drawered spicebox
 my grandma had
Held herbs grown in rich
 garden earth.
And for India spices she was
 always glad,
For she loved sweet fragrances
 on the hearth.

The old, iron Dutch oven
 with heaviest lid
Could never quite keep
 spicy aromas within.
For stews were the best
 that Grandmother did,
With a dot of each spice
 from a spicebox bin.

Rosemary and thyme,
 sweet marjoram and bay,
A wee dash of allspice and
 nutmeg a pinch.
"Appeals to my nose," I've oft
 heard her say.
Her spicebox stews were
 a delectable cinch.

And on the Saturday's usual,
   big baking day,
When pies, cookies, cakes,
   and breads were baked,
The beloved spicebox certainly
   held full sway.
For "too hot" savory sweets
   my heart had ached.

Then when the harvest time
   of year came near,
My grandma's spicebox bins
   would ne'er o'erflow,
For in almost everything "put up"
   so bright and clear,
She used the spice that
   made it good, I know!

So if perchance an old spicebox
   should you see,
With its many drawers and
   lingering scents,
Just try to think of all the things
   it used to be
To one who daily used
   each tiny bin's contents.

—Helen Gingrich Knowlton

Nostalgic Fragrance

Years ago, Grandmother knew
   how to save
The lavish gifts summer so freely gave,
Capturing the romance
   of flowers and sun
(A compensation for work well done).
She gathered rose petals
   in morning dew,
Rosemary, lavender and violets, too,
Drying them carefully in friendly shade,
Then, with roots and spices,
   she deftly made
A blend of summer captured to bring
A wealth of sun-laced remembering.
This haunting fragrance
   from another day
Was Grandmother's rose jar potpourri.

— Johanna Ter Wee

LEGACIES

Lineage

My grandmothers were strong.
They followed plows and bent to toil.
They moved through fields sowing seed.
They touched earth and grain grew.
They were full of sturdiness and singing.
My grandmothers were strong.

My grandmothers are full of memories,
Smelling of soap and onions
    and wet clay
With veins rolling roughly
    over quick hands.
They have many clean words to say.
My grandmothers were strong.
Why am I not as they?

—Margaret Walker

It would be more honorable to our
distinguished ancestors to praise them
in words less, but in deeds to imitate
them more.

—Horace Mann

My Favorite Story

My favorite story, dear Grandma,
Isn't one that you read to me
From a fairy tale or a picture book
Or a rhyme from the nursery—
It's one that you told
From your very heart,
Written deep in your memory.

You told me of two special people,
Who married a long while ago,
And how their love for each other
Made a little family grow,
And their children became
Aunts and uncles—
And a parent that I've come to know.

So what you told me, dear Grandma,
Was a part of our own history,
For the wonderful tale you related
Was the story of our family tree—
A moving, unique, and precious account
No one else could have given to me.

—*Jill Wolf*

Inheritance

China cupboards filled with cups
   of memories,
A piano that played in the days
   before me,
Secret drawers that hold
   my parents' past,
All these are here for me to see
And so piece together what
   has gone before
To understand the people who
   once walked these halls.

For in the home
   my grandmother created,
I find the beginnings of the love
   I have inherited.

—Lois Wyse

Some of the world's best educators
are grandparents.

— *Charles W. Shedd*

In many parts of the world, grandmothers are considered experts, and a young mother takes it for granted that when she has a question about her baby or needs a little help . . . she'll ask her mother.

—*Dr. Benjamin Spock*

In the effort to give good and comforting answers to the young questioners whom we love, we very often arrive at good and comforting answers for ourselves.

—*Ruth Goode*

If the very old will remember, the very young will listen.

—*Chief Dan George*

I don't go along with all this talk of a generation gap. We're all contemporaries. There is only a difference in memories, that's all.

—*W. H. Auden*

Grandma told me all about it,
Told me so I couldn't doubt it,
How she danced,
    my grandma danced;
    long ago . . .

—*Mary Mapes Dodge*

We must always have old
memories and young hopes.

—*Arsène Houssaye*

Age is opportunity no less
Than youth itself, though
    in another dress;
And as the evening twilight
    fades away,
The sky is filled with stars,
    invisible by day.

—*Henry Wadsworth Longfellow*

It is one of nature's ways that we often
feel closer to distant generations than to
the generation immediately preceding us.
— *Igor Stravinsky*

The Spinning Wheel

Maybe 'twas a happy day
When Grandma spun the hours away,
For thus within the old homespun
Is woven the spinner's quiet fun.

And then by the firelight's mellow glow
She never sat in idle woe,
But with woollen yarn so neatly spun
Knitted socks and mittens for everyone.

Or, if the weaving loom stood near,
The shuttles flew, and one could hear
The steady thump of the
    leachbar's shove,
And Grandma was wrapt
    in her work of love.

—*Helen Gingrich Knowlton*

Grandmother's Quilt

Nothing that anyone ever has built
Can even compare to
    Grandmother's quilt;
Only the wisest of hearts understands
The patience and skill that
    guided her hands.

With flowers and birds,
    with diamonds and squares,
She stitched a design in what cloth
    she could spare;
In yellow and green, in red, white,
    and blue,
From rags she made riches—
    and rainbows, too.

Like a puzzle with pieces for which
    she would search,
Like the stained-glass window
    in a country church,
A picture of life is transformed
    by her quilt,
More precious than anything
    anyone built.

—Jill Wolf